Revelation Revisited

Volume 4

Revelation Revisited

The Seven Bowls of God's Wrath

And

Babylon the Great

DR. JEAN NORBERT AUGUSTIN

(DD, DMM)

ACKNOWLEDGMENT

Unless stated otherwise, all Scriptures quoted in this book are from the World English Bible (WEB) thanks to the courtesy of Mr. Michael Johnson, chief editor.

EPIGRAPHS

"One of the seven angels who had the seven bowls came and spoke with me, saying, "Come here. I will show you the judgment of the great prostitute who sits on many waters, with whom the kings of the earth committed sexual immorality, and those who dwell in the earth were made drunken with the wine of her sexual immorality." (Revelation 17:12).

"I heard another voice from heaven, saying, "Come forth, my people, out of her, that you have no participation in her sins, and that you don't receive of her plagues,

for her sins have reached to the sky, and God has remembered her iniquities." (Revelation 18:4-5).

Table of Contents

PREFACE

In Volume 1, we looked at the Prologue of the Book of Revelation and we studied the Letters addressed to the seven Churches in Asia. In Volume 2, we studied the Seven Seals Judgments.

In Volume 3, our focus was on the Seven Trumpets Judgments.

In Volume 4, we are now going to examine the Seven Bowls of God's Wrath and Babylon the Great. The Book of Revelation containing a number of symbols and being written partly in figurative language, we do not claim to be able to explain everything in the vision.

However, in giving the vision to the apostle John, the Risen Jesus instructed him to write down everything to show to His servants things that were going to happen in the end times.

With the assistance of the Holy Spirit, we have, in all modesty, tried to explain whatever is possible and give to the reader an idea of what lies in store for mankind.

Our prayer is that, after having read this book in conjunction with *"Revelation"* in the Bible, the reader take a wise decision.

CHAPTER 1

REVELATION 15

"**1**I saw another great and marvelous sign in the sky: seven angels having the seven last plagues, for in them God's wrath is finished.

2 I saw something like a sea of glass mixed with fire, and those who overcame the beast, and his image, and the number of his name, standing on the sea of glass, having harps of God.

3 They sang the song of Moses, the servant of God, and the song of the Lamb, saying, "Great and marvelous are your works, Lord God, the Almighty; Righteous and true are your ways, you King of the nations.

_4_ *Who wouldn't fear you, Lord, And glorify your name? For you only are holy. For all the nations will come and worship before you. For your righteous acts have been revealed.*

_5_ *After these things I looked, and the temple of the tent of the testimony in heaven was opened.*

_6_ *The seven angels who had the seven plagues came out from the temple, clothed with pure, bright linen, and wearing golden sashes around their breasts.*

_7_ *One of the four living creatures gave to the seven angels seven golden bowls full of the wrath of God, who lives forever and ever.*

_8_ *The temple was filled with smoke from the glory of God, and from his power. No one was able to enter into the temple, until the seven plagues of the seven angels would be finished."*

The apostle John now sees seven angels ready to execute God's final series of seven judgments. People, left after the Rapture, have become so unrepentant and so rebellious that the only thing they can now expect is the Almighty's wrath.

People wonder how a God who is said to be god and merciful can manifest wrath. Some say that wrath is incompatible with God's character. Others base themselves upon such apparent contradictions to disbelieve and resort, instead, to atheism.

Yes, God is a merciful God. The Bible says that His mercy endures forever.[1]

Has He not, in His infinite mercy, offered to us His only begotten Son, Jesus, as a sacrifice to expiate all our sins?

Has He not offered us His infinite Grace – that gift that not a single human being deserves, can buy or can acquire by whatever means he may have?

---

[1] Psalm 100:5.

Has He not raised Jesus from the dead and sat him at His right hand to be our Advocate and sole Mediator between Him and us?[2]

Has He not sent Jesus to the world to proclaim a period of grace – a truce during which time the worst sinner can be accepted by God through repentance and accepting Jesus as sole Saviour and Redeemer?

Yes, the merciful God is also capable of manifesting wrath. But not for just any reason! His wrath is His most ultimate – pleonasm intentional – reaction to man's rebelliousness and ungodliness.

The apostle Paul also mentions God's wrath in his Epistle to the Romans:

18 "For the wrath of God is revealed from heaven against all ungodliness and unrighteousness of men, who hinder the truth in unrighteousness,

19 because that which is known by God is revealed in them, for God revealed it to them.

---

20 For the invisible things of him since the creation of the world are clearly seen, being perceived through the things that are made, even his everlasting power and divinity; that they may be without excuse.

21 Because, knowing God, they didn't glorify him as God, neither gave thanks, but became vain in their reasoning, and their senseless heart was darkened.

22 Professing themselves to be wise, they became fools,

23 and traded the glory of the incorruptible God for the likeness of an image of corruptible man, and of birds, and four-footed animals, and creeping things". [3]

In these Scriptures, Paul says how, right from the beginning of Creation, God has revealed His existence. There cannot be a creation without a Creator. It would be absurd to believe the opposite!

---

[3] Romans 1:18-23.

The sun, the moon, the stars, the times and the seasons – all testify to the existence of a Creator.

But what has man done in his supposed wisdom? Instead of worshipping the Creator, he has worshipped the creation! And he still does, in spite of all the technological advances of the modern era! Instead of worshipping the eternal and incorruptible God, he has resorted to worshipping corruptible things!

Notice, in the above Scriptures, the gradual spiritual degradation of man. In lieu of worshipping God, he has begun to worship (1) man, (2) birds, (3), four-footed animals and (4) creeping things! See the downward trend!

That is a direct and frontal violation of the first two Commandments[4]. Remember how the LORD's wrath burst in the desert of the Sinai when the people of Israel, with the complicity of Aaron – Moses's brother –

---

[4] Exodus 20:3-4.

made themselves a golden calf which they worshipped! Seeing the abomination, Moses's anger grew such that he smashed to pieces the tablets on which God had written the Decalogue with His own fingers!

In the Scriptures from Romans, how could the Almighty bear to see man, created in His own image, fall so low as to worship beasts and creeping things?

In reaction to that, God reveals His wrath!

The rest of chapter 1 of Romans gives us a graphic picture of what the consequences of man's foolishness are. Therein lie the fundamental explanation of the corrupt situation our world finds itself in.

"Exodus" also mentions God's wrath. After He had set the people of Israel free from slavery in Egypt, Moses improvised and sang a song to glorify and magnify the Almighty. He was joined in the rejoicing by Aaron's sister Miriam and all the women playing their tambourines and dancing.

The reason behind such a joyful rejoicing was the mighty work the LORD had wrought to set His people free.

In his song, Moses said:

"In the greatness of your excellency, you overthrow those who rise up against you: You send forth your wrath. It consumes them as stubble".[5]

But, let's go back to Revelation 15.

Simultaneously with that awe-inspiring sight of the seven angels – God's hitmen – the apostle John sees a glorious spectacle: a sea of glass mixed with fire! Standing on that magnificent sea, are those who conquered the Beast and the number of his name.

In *"Revelation Revisited Volume 3"*, we examined the subject of the Beast and the number of his name. The Beast is mentioned in Revelation 13:1 as *"the beast coming out of the sea"*. It's the Antichrist that causes havoc during the Great Tribulation.

____

[5] Exodus 15:7.

As for those who conquered him, it's obviously Jesus – riding a white horse - and his army, as we shall see in the next Volume.[6]

But, see that sharp contrast: the seven angels are about to be handed seven bowls full of God's unadulterated wrath while those who are standing on the sea of glass hold harps of God! On one hand, the worst calamities possible are about to be poured onto the world; on the other hand, harps are ready to accompany songs to the glory of the Almighty!

Indeed, those standing on the sea of glass, burst out singing the song of Moses and the song of the Lamb – that is, Jesus.

In the song, they praise the Almighty for His mighty works and for the truthfulness of His ways, calling Him *"King of the nations"*. All nations will have to come and worship before Him for He is holy and His acts are righteous.

To say that the Almighty's acts are righteous is tantamount to saying that, even when He

---

[6] Revelation 19:11.

reveals His wrath, He is right and just. No matter what He does, His acts are always justified.

Now eminently serious things are about to happen.

When the people of Israel had been set free from Egyptian bondage, God gave to Moses detailed instructions for the construction of a Tabernacle so that He could live among them.

The Tabernacle was called *"mishkân"* in Hebrew, that is a residence or a dwelling place.[7] It was to be a portable tent in which sacrifices would be offered for the expiation of sin, and in which the Almighty would be worshipped. However, that tent was movable for it had to accompany the Israelites all during their wanderings in the desert until they reached Canaan, the Promised Land.

---

[7] Britannica, The Editors of Encyclopaedia. "Tabernacle". Encyclopedia Britannica, 13 Dec. 2023, https://www.britannica.com/topic/Tabernacle. Accessed 6 February 2024.

When their wanderings were over and they settled in Canaan, they no longer needed a portable Tabernacle; they now needed a fixed place of worship. God, therefore, inspired King David to build a Temple where sacrifices could be offered and where He could be worshipped.

However, it was his son, King Solomon, who, eventually, built the Temple.

The Tabernacle and the Temple were built on the same model. They both had three sections: the outer court, the Holy Place and the Most Holy Place – the Holy of Holies.

The name, itself, tells us that the Holy of Holies was, by far, the most important and the most sacred compartment of the Tabernacle and of the Temple.

Indeed, while the people stood in the outer Court, the Priest could enter the Holy Place. But only the High Priest was allowed to enter the Holy of Holies – and, even then, only once a year, on *"Yom Kippur"*, the Day of Atonement!

Should anybody else enter therein – or even the High Priest on another day – they would be struck dead! Indeed, the Holy of Holies was a place of paramount sacredness and holiness: it was there that the Almighty manifested His Holy Presence through the Ark of the Covenant.[8]

Now, the Holy of Holies in the Tabernacle and in the Temple was an earthly representation of Heaven – a type of the Heavenly Archetype[9].

But, once He had accomplished atonement for our sins, Jesus ascended to Heaven and sat at the right hand side of the Father on His Heavenly Throne. In so doing, He has entered into another Tabernacle not made by the hands of man as the earthly Tabernacle was.

"**11** *But Christ having come as a high priest of the coming good things, through the*

---

[8] Hebrews 8:6-7.
[9] Hebrews 8:5.

greater and more perfect tent, not made with hands, that is to say, not of this creation,

12 nor yet through the blood of goats and calves, but through his own blood, entered in once for all into the Holy Place, having obtained eternal redemption". [10]

The reason I have been speaking about the Tabernacle – both in its earthly form and in its Heavenly form – is to show how glorious but ominous the spectacle that offers itself to the apostle John now.

Indeed, the Heavenly Tabernacle is opened. This verb in the passive voice implies that the Heavenly Tent did not open on its own: Somebody opened it! Who? The Scriptures do not say explicitly who. But it must have been a most eminent Personage, being given where He is and the authority He has to open the Tent!

---

[10] Hebrews 9:11-12.

And the seven angels appear! They have been commissioned to cast upon planet Earth the seven bowls of God's wrath.

Their appearance is glorious and majestic. They are *"clothed with pure, bright linen, and wearing golden sashes around their breasts"*. Their impressive appearance tells of their eminence and of the mission they have been assigned. They must definitely belong to a higher class of angels.

They are then given the seven bowls filled to the brim with God's wrath. Some versions of the Bible use the word "vials" instead of "bowls". That does not make a big difference – except that bowls are deeper than vials - insofar as both are used as symbols in the figurative sense. What is important, however, is the content of these receptacles: God's wrath!

When the seven bowls are handed over to the seven angels, a smoke fills the Heavenly Temple, manifesting the Almighty's Holy Presence and Glory.

That is not without reminding us of a similar occurrence during the dedication of the Jerusalem Temple. On that memorable day, the glory of the LORD manifested itself in such a visible and almost tangible way that the priest could not remain on his feet to do the service![11]

Likewise, now that the seven angels hold the seven bowls of God's wrath, nobody can enter the Heavenly Temple as long as the seven plagues are not over.

On the Cross, Jesus shed His blood to the very last drop; now God's wrath must be poured till not a single drop is left!

---

[11] 2 Chronicles 5:14.

CHAPTER 2

REVELATION 16

<u>1</u> *"I heard a loud voice out of the temple, saying to the seven angels, "Go and pour out the seven bowls of the wrath of God on the earth!"*

<u>2</u> *The first went, and poured out his bowl into the earth, and it became a harmful and evil sore on the men who had the mark of the beast, and who worshiped his image.*

<u>3</u> *The second angel poured out his bowl into the sea, and it became blood as of a dead man. Every living thing in the sea died."* (Revelation 16:1-3).

Now trouble really and seriously begins for the world. God's wrath reaches its climax and the world is about to witness the worst calamities ever.

The prophet Zephaniah, prophesying against Judah, warned of terrible days about to be seen in the kingdom in the following terms:

"15 *That day is a day of wrath, a day of distress and anguish, a day of trouble and ruin, a day of darkness and gloom, a day of clouds and blackness*".[12]

If, in the days of Zephaniah, the day of God's wrath was described in such gloomy and gruesome terms, we can imagine how much more terrible and more … apocalyptic His wrath will be now!

In the Olivet Discourse, Jesus gave this warning: "*for then will be great oppression, such as has not been from the beginning of the world until now, no, nor ever will be.*[13]

---

[12] Zephaniah 1:15.
[13] Matthew 24:21.

If Zephaniah's prophecy was addressed to the kingdom of Judah for a limited period, Jesus's warning, on the contrary, is directly related to the end-times and to the whole world. He promises that the oppression in the end-times will be such as has never been seen nor such as will ever be seen!

That alone is enough to give us a hint as to will befall the world in those days!

With the pouring out of the bowl of the first angel upon the earth, its content becomes a terrible sore on the body of everyone who worshipped the Beast – that is, the Antichrist – and his image.

That must be an awful, ugly and painful skin disease – much more handicapping than what Satan stuck Job with.[14] In Job's case, the skin ulcer affected only one man – a man loved by God, who was being tested.

But, during the Great Tribulation, the sore will affect all those who will be worshipping the Beast. In other words, virtually all that

---

[14] Job 1.

will have been left of humanity after the Rapture and the Seal and Trumpet judgments, that we examined in volumes 2 and 3.

When the second angel pours out the content of his bowl upon the sea, all its water turns into blood. Consequently, all marine animal and plant life dies. Not only is the sea a great source of food for human beings, but it is also a major source of oxygen.

We remember how water turning into blood was one of the plagues that the Almighty sent upon Egypt to break Pharaoh's pride and demonstrate His superiority over the Egyptian gods.[15]

The third angel is commissioned to pour out his bowl upon all rivers and springs of water. Their waters, too, turn into blood. Thus, there is no fresh water fish to provide food to people and vital drinking water is considerably depleted or simply no longer available!

---

[15] Exodus 7:20-21.

Consequently, mankind finds himself without food and without water.

Recently, we witnessed live on television the dire situation in Gaza during the war between Israel and Hamas. We saw how people ran short of food and water – among other things – how they starved and how they threw themselves over food supplies brought by humanitarian organizations.

In Gaza, terrible as it was, that was only a regional situation and food supplies and water – though scanty – were still provided. But, with the plagues we are examining here, the very sources of essential life supporting foods will be annihilated! What a hellish time to be living in!

Lest those falling under those judgments or anybody else should think that they are far too severe and unjust, an angel established over the waters justifies God's actions.

He declares that God is the Holy One and His judgments are just. Those upon whom His judgments fall well deserve them: since they shed the blood of God's saints, it is quite in order that they be now given blood to drink. Since they rejected the One who came to give living water – Jesus Christ[16] – they chose to worship the Beast, let them now have blood to drink, instead!

There comes a voice from the altar that also justifies the Almighty's judgments.

We may wonder how can an inanimate thing like an altar speak. But, let us remember Jesus's entry into Jerusalem. The crowd shouted:

"Hosanna to the son of David! Blessed is he who comes in the name of the Lord! Hosanna in the highest!"[17]

When the crowd was scandalized and asked Him to order His disciples to shut up, Jesus answered:

"He answered them, "I tell you that if these were silent, the stones would cry out."[18]

---

[16] John 7:37-39.
[17] Matthew 21:9.
[18] Luke 19:40.

If stones can speak, why can the Heavenly altar not speak?

And if Abel's blood can speak, why shouldn't the Heavenly altar be able to speak?[19]

The fourth angel now pours out his bowl upon the sun. The heat of the sun is increased and men's bodies are scorched. In all logic, they ought to have repented and asked the Almighty, who has authority over the plagues, to forgive them and stop the plagues.

Remember how the repentant thief, crucified beside Jesus, obtained from Him the promise of Paradise[20]. But those worshipping the Beast during the Great Tribulation are under such satanic subjection that they have no thought of repentance.

The fifth angel has for assignment to pour out his bowl upon the throne of the Beast! Here we see an attack targeting directly the Beast!

---

[19] Hebrews 12:24.
[20] Luke 23:39-43.

It is a bold and audacious attack against the one who is the Mastermind behind all the evils the world is committing.

To better understand what is going on, let us draw a parallel with an event the world witnessed just a few months ago.

We remember how, in retaliation to Hamas's terror attack in September 2023, Israel invaded Northern Gaza to destroy Hamas's base of operation. We saw on television how brutal and merciless the retaliation was!

What will happen when the day comes for the fifth angel to pour out his bowl of God's wrath upon the throne of the Beast! Compared to this, the invasion of Northern Gaza will seem quite meaningless. In his vision – his time travel – the apostle John has already seen what it will look like.

The kingdom of the Beast turns to complete darkness. Obviously, God is Light; His Archenemy is, therefore, darkness. Darkness was one of the ten plagues that God struck Egypt with during the tug-of-war between

Moses and Pharaoh for the liberation of the Israelites.[21]

As in the aftermath of the fourth bowl judgment, the people do not repent. Instead, they gnaw their tongues and ostentatiously speak blasphemy against God!

Their reaction defies all logic. How absurd, we may ask. But, being worshippers of the Beast, they must have been possessed not by demons – but by Satan, himself! Remember how Satan entered into Judas just as he took the piece of bread from the plate at the Last Supper![22] Thus being Satan possessed, he went straightaway to betray Jesus.

Once people fall prey to Satan and allow themselves to be taken possession of, there is no telling where they will end!

Now the situation gains even greater momentum and the situation grows even worse.

---

[21] Exodus 10:22-23.
[22] Luke 22:3; John 13:27.

Indeed, the sixth angel pours out his bowl on the Euphrates.

In the case of the third angel, we remember he poured his bowl upon all rivers and springs of water. As a consequence, their water turned into blood so that all animal and plant life therein was destroyed.

In the case of the Euphrates, however, the situation is completely different. Its water does not turn to blood: it dries up!

The Euphrates, indeed, is a unique River. It is quite different from all other rivers. According to the Bible, it has a very long story. Not only is it a great and unique River because of its origin, but also because of the role it will, one day, play towards the end of human history!

Let us see something about this River.

The Euphrates starts in Turkey, runs through Syria then to Iraq where it joins its sister

River, the Tigris. They end their course in the Persian Gulf.[23]

We first see the Euphrates in … Genesis, the book of the beginnings! There, we learn that there was a river which watered the Garden of Eden. Then that river separated into four rivers: Pishon, Gihon, Hiddekel and … Euphrates![24]

It makes us wonder when we realize that our very first ancestors, Adam and Eve, must have drunk of its water!

The region where it is situated is called Mesopotamia – the land between two rivers: the Euphrates and the Tigris. That region is also known as the Fertile Crescent.

That name, itself, is enough to tell us that it was a very rich and luxuriant region.

Mesopotamia is the region where the great Patriarch Abram – later called Abraham – lived. Again, we wonder when we realize

---

[23] https://en.wikipedia.org/wiki/Euphrates. Accessed 2/6/2024.
[24] Genesis 2:10-14.

that he must have led his flocks to drink of that water. No wonder his flocks grew fat and multiplied and the old man prospered!

The Euphrates is a unique River – totally different from all other rivers.

Throughout the Bible – from Genesis to Revelation – we see it mentioned. It is so exceptional that it is often mentioned only as *"the River"* or *"the great River"*.

In the Old Testament, it is very often used as a marker of space – a boundary, as it were. Let us see a few examples.

When the Almighty made a covenant with Abraham with regard to the Promised Land, He used the Euphrates as a boundary:

"In that day Yahweh made a covenant with Abram, saying, "To your seed have I given this land, from the river of Egypt to the great river, the river Euphrates" [25].

---

[25] Genesis 15:18.

King Solomon's kingdom, it is said, extended to that River:

"Solomon ruled over all the kingdoms from the River to the land of the Philistines, and to the border of Egypt: they brought tribute, and served Solomon all the days of his life"[26].

Prophesying over the lost Israelites, God promised that they would, one day, return and that their settlement would extend to the River [Euphrates]:

"In that day they will come to you from Assyria and the cities of Egypt, And from Egypt even to the River, And from sea to sea, And mountain to mountain"[27].

In *Revelation,* we already saw mention of the Euphrates[28]. During the Seven Trumpet judgments, when the sixth angel blew his trumpet, he was ordered to release the four angels bound to the River:

---

26 1 Kings 2:21.
27 Micah 7:12.
28 Revelation Revisited, Volume3.

"The sixth angel sounded. I heard a voice from the horns of the golden altar which is before God, saying to the sixth angel who had one trumpet, "Free the four angels who are bound at the great river Euphrates[29].

Once released, the four angels will have for mission to exterminate one third of what will have been left of mankind.

Thus, we see how important the role of the Euphrates is in God's Plan.

Let us get back to the Bowl judgments and see how things evolve.

As we said above, it is the mission of the sixth angel to pour out his bowl upon the Euphrates. It is surprising to note that in both – the Trumpet judgments and the Bowl judgments – that it is the sixth angel who is concerned with the Euphrates!

---

[29] Revelation 9:13-14.

When the third angel poured out his bowl upon all rivers and springs of water, all their water turned into blood.

Amazingly, when the sixth angel poured out his bowl over the Euphrates, its water dried up!

This happened so that the River became a way for all the kings coming "from the sunrise".

Next, John sees three frog-like creatures coming out of the mouth of the Beast and of the mouth of the false prophet. In fact, those are demonic spirits that perform all kinds of miracles to deceive mankind.

Those demonic spirits then go to gather all the kings of the north to incite them to wage war. That war will be the ultimate war that will put an end to mankind's history.

The Bible tells us that the devil can disguise himself into an angel of light. [30]If such is the case, how much more can he disguise himself

---

[30] 2 Corinthians 11:14.

as vile and unclean beings! It would appear that he is so cunning that his disguise depends on circumstances. He knows how to adapt himself to situations.

Indeed, in the Garden of Eden, he took the semblance of a serpent because, as a serpent, he could easily wriggle his way across the lush grass of the Garden, unnoticed.

Now, in *"Revelation"* 16, we see him using frog-like demonic spirits to gather all the kings of the world to wage war. Among the plagues God sent over Egypt to force the Pharaoh to set the Israelite captives free, there was one characterized by an invasion and infestation of frogs. When millions of those creatures died, we can imagine what stench filled the whole country![31].

But not only are frogs foul and unclean creatures: they are also amphibians! In other words, they have the ability to move in water as well as on land. Thus, the frog-like demonic spirits will be able to easily and

---

[31] Exodus 8:1-14.

quickly move from the north to the south, from the east to the west to assemble all the kings of the world to go to war.

This war will be the ultimate war. It is called here *"the war of the great day of God, the Almighty"*. It represents the limit of the Almighty's longsuffering – the culmination of His wrath!

Remember, during the Great Tribulation, God is still sending out His Word to bring people back to Him:

"I saw another angel flying in mid heaven, having an eternal gospel to proclaim to those who dwell on the earth, and to every nation, tribe, language, and people".[32]

Mankind is, at this stage, without excuse! It's time for His legitimate wrath to be poured out upon the world with maximum potency!

However, Jesus, in His mercy, has yet another warning to give to mankind:

---

[32] Revelation 14:6.

""Behold, I come like a thief. Blessed is he who watches, and keeps his clothes, so that he doesn't walk naked, and they see his shame"[33].

The place of that mega-gathering is Harmageddon.[34]

As the seventh angel pours out his bowl into the air, a voice is heard coming out of the Heavenly Temple, saying: *"It is done!"*

What a dramatic and ominous shout!

This reminds us how, when Jesus gave out his last breath on the Cross, He said: *"It's finished."*

For Him, everything the Father had sent Him to do had been fully and successfully accomplished. The last drop of His blood had been shed: man's redemption had been paid for.

Now, with that shout of *"It is done!"*, God's patience had reached its limit. He had done

---

[33] Revelation 16:15.
[34] Also spelt "Armageddon". Situated in the valley of Megiddo in Northern Israel.

everything possible to turn mankind away from the devil and turn it to Him, but all to no avail!

All that is left for mankind to expect now is the last drops of His wrath! And those are the most concentrated drops of His wrath – just like the last drops at the bottom of the bottle of wine. They have been lying there the longest and so are the most fermented and the most concentrated.

As the seventh angel poured out his bowl, loud sounds were heard, thunders rolled, lightings flashed and a great earthquake burst. No such thing had ever been seen since man first existed on earth!

Notice the plural in "thunders" and "lightings". With the loud sounds and the mighty earthquake, we can only vaguely imagine what commotion and havoc that caused!

Every island fled, mountains disappeared! The cities of the nations fell. Hailstones –

weighing one talent[35] each – fell from the sky on men.

In their madness, men blasphemed God and cursed Him because of the hail plague.

We remember that hail storm was also one of the plagues God punished Egypt with for not letting His people go.[36]

Imagine hail stones that heavy falling upon people! Logic tells us that they ought to repent and plead for God's mercy. But the Beast whom they worshipped had robbed them of all power of reasoning.

The same thing happened when the fourth angel poured out his bowl upon the sun and people's skin was scorched.

Another situation where we saw such madness was when one of the two criminals crucified beside Jesus blasphemed Him, saying: *"If you are the Christ, save yourself and us!"* [37]

---

[35] 100 pounds.
[36] Exodus 9:18-35.
[37] Luke 23:39.

Even the passers-by blasphemed, saying:

"Ha! You who destroy the temple, and build it in three days,

save yourself, and come down from the cross!" [38]

God is Light. When people reject Jesus, the Light of the world, they end up walking in utter darkness and fall victim to folly![39]

Although these calamities strike the whole world, one city, in particular, is singled out: Babylon!

Indeed, its lot is going to be different from that of every other city. It is called here *"the great city"*[40]. Her evil doings are brought to God's remembrance.

Of course, God being omniscient, does not have to be reminded of anything. It's just a figure of speech, a literary way of expressing an idea.

---

[38] Mark 15:29-30.
[39] John 8:12.
[40] Revelation 18:21.

If God is to be reminded of something –
especially sins - He must, first, have
forgotten it. But, does He ever forget?

In a covenant made with the house of Israel,
God says: *"I will forgive their iniquity, and
their sin will I remember no more"*[41]

*"I, even I, am he who blots out your
transgressions for my own sake; and I will
not remember your sins"*[42]

*"For I will be merciful to their
unrighteousness. I will remember their sins
and lawless deeds no more."*[43]

So, the above Scriptures prove, beyond the
shadow of a doubt, that, once God has
forgiven our sins, He remembers them no
more. He has blotted them completely!

How come, then, that He remembers
Babylon's sins? Has He not blotted them?

---

[41] Jeremiah 31:34.
[42] Isaiah 43:25.
[43] Hebrews 8:12.

If He remembers, Babylon's sins must, therefore, be indelible – so abominable as to resist blotting!

In consequence, God has reserved for her *"the cup of the wine of the fierceness of his wrath"*![44]

Thus, it's Babylon that's going to take the brunt of the Almighty's wrath.

In the next chapter, we shall examine more closely the subject of Babylon.

---

[44] Revelation 16:19.

CHAPTER 3

BABYLON – OLD AND NEW

Chapter 16 of *"Revelation"* ends with mention of the fate awaiting Babylon, the great city. As we saw, it's the city that takes the brunt of God's wrath. To her will be given *"the cup of the wine of the fierceness of his wrath"*. [45]

We wonder why such a terrible fate is reserved for this city. What wrong or wrongs she may have done? Who or what is Babylon, in the first place?

Chapter 17 answers these questions and many others. Although it provides us with much information about this city, this chapter is, nevertheless, one of the most intriguing

---

[45] Revelation 16:19.

and the most debated chapters of the entire Bible.

As we know, the Old Testament is full of types – shadows that prefigure certain realities revealed in the New Testament.

The name "Babylon" reminds us of the Tower of Babel of old, mentioned in Genesis, the book of the beginnings and of the captivity period of the Israelites under Nebuchadnezzar.

Founded about 2300 B.C, Babylon stood along the banks of the Euphrates in Mesopotamia which is modern day Iraq. Under Hammurabi whose reign extended from 1792 B.C to 1750 B.C, Babylon grew into a great military power. It even had its legal system thanks to Hammurabi's Code. Among the seven wonders of the ancient world were the hanging gardens of Babylon.

Babylon was also renowned for its hanging gardens – one of the wonders of the ancient world.[46]

The Bible records the building of the Tower of Babel by Nimrod. Having grown exceedingly proud, the Babylonians, in their folly, started to build a tower so high it would reach the heavens. But God thwarted their plan by multiplying their language into diverse ones. Unable to communicate, they had to give up their mad enterprise.[47]

---

[46] Article Title: Babylon

Author: History.com Editors

Website Name: HISTORY

URL: https://www.history.com/topics/ancient-middle-east/babylon

Date Accessed: February 8, 2024

Publisher: A&E Television Networks

Last Updated: May 31, 2023

Original Published Date: February 2, 2018

[47] Genesis 11:1-9.

Under the rule of the wicked king Nebuchadnezzar, during the sixth century B.C, the Babylonians captured the people of Juda and took them into captivity. After seventy years of captivity, they were allowed to return to their homeland by the Persian king Cyrus the Great into whose hands Babylon had fallen.[48]

Among the captives were none other than the prophet Daniel and his three companions: Hananiah, Mishael and Azariah. Their names, however, were changed to Meshach, Shadrach and Abed-nego, respectively.[49]

These brief notes about the Babylon of the Old Testament give us already an idea of what we are about to discover about Babylon in *"Revelation"* chapter 17.

This is not to say that the Babylon of *"Revelation"* is an exact replica of the Old Testament Babylon. If the latter was

---

[48] Daniel 9
[49] Daniel 1:6-7.

essentially a political power, the former has more the characteristics of a religious system.

Let us look more closely at chapter 17 to see what and how much we can gather from it about Babylon, the great city.

CHAPTER 4

REVELATION 17

"<u>*1*</u> *One of the seven angels who had the seven bowls came and spoke with me, saying, "Come here. I will show you the judgment of the great prostitute who sits on many waters,*

<u>*2*</u> *with whom the kings of the earth committed sexual immorality, and those who dwell in the earth were made drunken with the wine of her sexual immorality."*

<u>*3*</u> *He carried me away in the Spirit into a wilderness. I saw a woman sitting on a scarlet-colored animal, full of blasphemous names, having seven heads and ten horns.*

<u>*4*</u> *The woman was dressed in purple and scarlet, and decked with gold and precious stones and pearls, having in her hand a*

golden cup full of abominations, even the unclean things of her sexual immorality,

5 and on her forehead a name written, "MYSTERY, BABYLON THE GREAT, THE MOTHER OF THE PROSTITUTES AND OF THE ABOMINATIONS OF THE EARTH."

6 I saw the woman drunken with the blood of the saints, and with the blood of the martyrs of Jesus. When I saw her, I wondered with great amazement.

7 The angel said to me, "Why do you wonder? I will tell you the mystery of the woman, and of the beast that carries her, which has the seven heads and the ten horns".

Now, one of the seven angels provided with the bowls of God's wrath invites the apostle John to come and see the judgment that has been reserved for Babylon. She is referred to here as *"the prostitute who sits on many waters"*.

First of all, we note the use of the definite article *"the"*. As opposed to the indefinite article *"a"*, "the" designates a specific *"prostitute"* – not just any random prostitute. This idea is reinforced by the qualifiers *"great"* and *"who sits on many waters"*.

It goes without saying that no person can sit on water – even less, a prostitute! It is clear that this is figurative language. The phrase *"many waters"* stands for great multitudes of people. In other words, the great prostitute has power over huge masses of people. She lords it over them. They are in complete subjection to her and answers her every beck and call. Her influence must be mighty!

Next, the appellation "prostitute" is … pregnant with meaning. It gives us the moral character of Babylon. She has to be immoral, impure, sensual and the like.

The angel announces already some of the crimes she has committed: all the kings of the earth have committed adultery with her and all the inhabitants of the world *"were made drunken with the wine of her sexual immorality*".[50]

The use of the passive voice here implies that the inhabitants of the world were victims of her "*wine of sexual immorality*"[51]: they were made to drink of it! This confirms what we said above – namely that she had them in completely subjection to her and lorded it over them!

In a much lesser degree, she reminds us of the Jezebel in the Church in Thyatira who taught God's servants to commit sexual immorality and eat food sacrificed to idols.[52]

The angel then takes John in the spirit to the wilderness: there the apostle sees a woman riding a weird animal. It is scarlet-coloured, has ten horns and seven horns and is covered with blasphemous names.

This beast looks very much like the one in "*Revelation*" 13:1. It came out of the sea and

---

[50] Revelation 17:4.
[51] Revelation 17: 4.
[52] Revelation 2: 20-23.

obtained its power, its authority and its throne from the dragon. This beast turned out to be the Antichrist.

And, here, John sees that woman sitting a similar beast – which, eventually, may turn out to be the same beast.

While the scarlet colour is reminiscent of blood, the blasphemous names with which the beast is covered clearly say that it opposes God Almighty.

The woman's appearance gives us additional information about her. She wears purple and scarlet garments, and is decked with gold, pearls and precious stones.

As we said above, the scarlet signifies blood. The purple, however, speaks of wealth, opulence, luxury, glamour.

We remember the selfish rich man, dressed in rich clothes and purple, in the Gospel. He daily feasted, never caring to give the least piece of bread to Lazarus, a poor beggar, covered with sores, sitting at his doorstep.

When both died, Lazarus was taken to Abraham's bosom – Paradise – by angels. The wicked rich man, on the contrary, was cast into fire which so burned him that he begged Father Abraham to send Lazarus over to him to dip his finger in water and appease his suffering.[53]

The book of Acts also mentions a rich woman called Lydia who traded in purple in the city of Thyatira. She was apparently a very rich lady. When she and her household believed and were baptized, she opened her house to the apostle Paul and his companions.[54]

Purple is also associated with high religious dignitaries and royalty. During important religious ceremonies and coronation ceremonies, which are celebrated in great pomp, we see a lot of purple.

---

[53] Full story in Luke 16:19-31.
[54] Acts 16:14-15.

The fact that the woman sitting on the beast is dressed in purple speaks of her high status and of her appurtenance to a religious system.

This is confirmed by the gold, the pearls and the precious stones she is decked with.

In her hand, she held a golden cup full of her abominations and sexual immorality.

One would imagine that a golden cup is supposed to contain pure things – even things of the highest purity! But here, the golden cup is full to the brim with the woman's sexual immorality and abominations! That tells us that her abominations and sexual immorality must have been of the highest and vilest order!

Did the woman commit adultery and other acts of immorality with humans only? The Scriptures say that *"even the unclean things of her sexual immorality, were made drunken with the wine of her sexual immorality"*.[55] What were those *"evil things"*? Did she

---

[55] Revelation 17:4.

commit bestiality, as well, or commit immoral acts with some alien creatures? The Scriptures do not further clarify this.

Nevertheless, the imagery of a woman – a prostitute, in addition! – holding a cup full of the wine of abominations and immorality with which she intoxicates humans and *"evil things"* brings to mind orgy of the worst sort!

"Revelation" was written during the reign of notorious Roman Emperors. Those were known for their overly sensual and immoral mode of life. Orgies during which food, drink and sex were indulged in unchecked were the order of the day.

The depicting of the woman mentioned in this chapter must have been clearly grasped by the people of John's day – very much like Jesus's audiences could easily connect with His parables! The description of the woman dressed in scarlet and purple must have shocked their imagination!

The further we proceed with our reading, the more we discover about the woman's personality.

We now see that she has an inscription on her forehead – and a most revealing one at that! The inscription presents her as:

"MYSTERY, BABYLON THE GREAT, THE MOTHER OF THE PROSTITUTES AND OF THE ABOMINATIONS OF THE EARTH."

In ancient Rome, prostitutes sometimes advertised their profession by wearing a headband bearing their names. Again, *"Revelation"* uses an imagery that evokes the day's reality to the people of that time. The description of the woman here speaks directly to the minds of the people so that it's easy for them to entertain not the shadow of a doubt about the woman's identity: she, personally, advertises herself as *"the mother of prostitutes and of the abominations of the earth"*!

By proclaiming herself as the *"mother"* of all the prostitutes and the abominations of the earth, she implies that she is the source of all the prostitution and abomination going on in the world. She is, in fact, the mastermind behind it all!

John then sees that the woman is drunk with the blood of the saints and of the martyrs of Jesus – that is, of all who are followers of Jesus and those who have been put to death for His cause.

Having reached this far, we can clearly see that this *"woman"* cannot be a real female human being! There are many facts stated in this portion of Scripture to prove what we are saying.

Let's see.

How can a prostitute – whether male or female – sit on many waters?

How can a prostitute indulge in prostitution with all the kings of the earth?

In the first place, she would need to have exceptional logistics to travel all over the world to reach out to the kings – unless all the kings of the world travelled to her love nest and that is most improbable! Last but not least, she would need to be admitted into the kings' presence and … accepted for her … services!

How could she ride a beast with seven heads and ten horns without it devouring her?

How could she be drunk with the blood of all the saints and of all the martyrs of Jesus? It's true that there are people practising witchcraft or in secret societies who do drink blood. But, none can logically drink as much blood as mentioned in these Scriptures! Neither is blood intoxicating!

It is, therefore, clear that the language used in relation to that woman is figurative. It's just a picture to illustrate all the evil being wrought by the devil and his agents – a picture that strikes the imagination! Don't they say that a picture is worth a thousand words?

So, if the prostitute is not a real woman, who or what is she?

"She" must personify a system – an organization whose evil influence and devilish actions extend to the whole world! Indeed, no single human being – male or female – can have influence of that magnitude and perform actions of that gravity on a worldwide scale!

As we proceed in our study, we will, undoubtedly, discover further evidence to shed more light on this woman.

When the apostle John sees her, he is struck with awe! Quite naturally so!

On the other hand, the angel – being a heavenly being – is not shocked at all. He is shocked only on seeing John … shocked! Instead, he informs the apostle that he will explain to him the mystery of the woman and of the beast with seven heads and ten horns.

The irony is that, in spite of the angel's explanation, what will follow remains one on the most difficult portions of the Bible. Certainly, the angel does clarify certain things by deciphering a few symbols mentioned here. But, to this day, there is no consensus among Bible scholars as to the precise referents designated by the symbols.

In all humility, I don't claim to be able to dogmatically explain what will follow. I will simply repeat what has already been said here and explain only what is explainable.

"The beast that you saw was, and is not; and is about to come up out of the abyss, and to go into destruction. Those who dwell on the earth will wonder, whose name has not been written in the book of life from the foundation of the world, when they see the beast, how that he was, and is not, and will come.

9 Here is the mind that has wisdom. The seven heads are seven mountains, on which the woman sits.

10 They are seven kings. Five have fallen, the one is, the other is not yet come. When he comes, he must continue a little while.

**11** The beast that was, and is not, is himself also an eighth, and is of the seven; and he goes to destruction".

Regarding the beast, he once existed, exists no more – as at the time _"Revelation"_ was written in the first century CE – and will reappear some time. He will come out of the abyss and go to his destruction.

The fact that he will come out of the abyss is enough to tell us that he is unquestionably of satanic origin and nature. The abyss is the bottomless pit into which demons, foul and unclean spirits are cast.

If the facts concerning his origin and his destination are fairly clear to understand, what is said about his past existence, his disappearance and his reappearing is more mind baffling!

Anyway, when he will reappear, those unsaved – whose names are not recorded in the Lamb's Book of Life – will wonder. Deceived by the forces of darkness, they will consider that as a feat and will worship him.

Verse 9 is a verse that has given rise to much controversy. The angel explains that the seven heads of the beast are seven mountains on which the woman sits.

Reference to seven mountains, at once, brings to our mind one city – Rome!

This is because it is common knowledge that Rome is the city built on seven hills. There was even a film titled *"Seven Hills of Rome"*[56] .

"Revelation" 17:9 mentions "mountains". If some commentators readily associate this verse with Rome, others argue that Rome does not have seven *"mountains"* but seven *"hills"*. For them, we should not be quick to associate this reference with Rome.

---

[56] Wikipedia: Release date: November 21, 1957 (Italy)

Directors: Roy Rowland, Mario Russo

Box office: 2.155 million USD

Distributed by: Metro-Goldwyn-Mayer, United Artists, Accessed 02/08/2024.

In a sense, they are right. But what other city has that singular characteristic? Should we really make a big issue of that debate over mountains versus hills when the Bible establishes allegories between elements much further apart such as we are seeing in this chapter, itself?

The seven hills of Rome are: Quirinal, Viminal, Capitoline, Esquiline, Palatine, Caelian and Aventine.[57]

Another difficulty arises when verse 9 tells us that the woman sits on the seven mountains.

As we said above, it is clear that the *"woman"* cannot be a literal woman. Otherwise, how could she sit on seven mountains or hills?

---

[57] Wikipedia: File: Seven Hills of Rome.Svg. In *Wikipedia.* https://commons.wikimedia.org/wiki/File:Seven_Hills_of_Rome.svg, Accessed 27.01.2024.

Besides, was the woman not sitting on many waters (v.1)? Was she not sitting on the beast (v.3)? How come she now sits on seven mountains (v.9)?

A literal woman cannot be sitting on so many things extending over such vast spaces like the "many waters" and the seven mountains!

Being given the expanse of the woman's influence, it would not be illogical to say that this word must refer to some sort of worldwide system or organization.

Now we come to yet another intriguing verse.

John is told that the seven heads are seven kings. Five have already gone and one still exists. The seventh is yet to come and, when he comes, he will reign for a short time only.

We remind readers that the situation described here relates to the times when the apostle John received the vision during the first century CE – around 95-96 CE.

There is so much controversy over this question of seven kings that I do not want to add to the confusion by commenting on that.

Indeed, some commentators take those seven kings to be seven Roman Emperors. But, even then, there is no consensus as to who the seven were. The problem is to know from what date to start counting the seven Emperors - what should be the starting point! Thus, various commentators come up with various names.

Among the names most commonly mentioned by commentators are Claudius, Nero, Otho, Galba, Vitellius, Vespasian, Titus, Nerva, Tiberius, Gaius, Caligula and Domitian.

Another cause of the dissension among commentators regarding the seven kings is that they do not all agree about the precise date of the writing of *"Revelation"*.

However, it is commonly agreed that Domitian was the Emperor reigning when *"Revelation"* was written.

Other commentators associate the seven kings with seven great kingdoms, instead. Those are supposed to be Egypt, Assyria, Babylonia, Persia, Greece, Rome – that was, then, in power – and a revival of the Roman Empire.

So, we see how diverse and conflicting are the views expressed about the seven kings of verse 10.

I, personally, uphold a principle: when God's Word is clear and straightforward, I take it at face value. But, when it is unclear or silent about an issue, I don't put into His mouth words He never uttered or bend His Word to make it fit my theology.

As for the king *"that was and is not"*, it is easy to identify him as the beast that came out of the sea and that had ten horns and seven heads. It had sustained *"a fatal wound"* that healed afterwards.[58]

The *"fatal wound"* that, miraculously healed, may refer to a "resurrection" wrought by

---

[58] Revelation 13: 1-3.

Satan to fake Jesus's resurrection. We discussed that in volume 2.

That beast may well be the eighth king mentioned in Revelation 17:11. He was originally one of the seven, died, then rose again – thus becoming the eighth king.

Next, the angel informs John that the ten horns are ten kings. However, these kings have not yet obtained their kingdom. They are, as it were, kings in waiting! They will receive their authority with the Beast. But their authority will be exercised during a short time only.

Many commentators are of the opinion that these ten kings in waiting will emanate from the European Union (EU).

Founded in 1957 by six countries, the European Union now comprises twenty-seven countries.[59] It is believed that, in the end times, the group will end up with ten countries that will become the ten kings of

---

[59] World Population Review, accessed 29 January 2024.

"*Revelation*". Or, maybe, ten of them will emerge as modern powers and play an important role in the apocalyptic tragedy about to be staged during the Great Tribulation.

Irrespective of what or who that tenth king will be, one thing is clearly stated here: "*it will go to destruction*"! (v.11).

There is, however, a great solidarity among them. They all have a single mind. In one accord, they give their power and authority to the Beast and, single-mindedly, they will wage war against the Lamb – that is, Jesus.

But, quite naturally, Jesus will defeat them all for He is the King of kings and the Lord of lords! His faithful and chosen ones will also participate and have a share in His victory.

In verse 1, we learned that the woman –the harlot – was sitting on "*many waters*". As we said above, no ordinary woman can achieve such a feat.

Indeed, we are now told that those *"many waters"* are, in fact, *"peoples, multitudes, nations, languages"*. In other words, the woman must be a representation of a worldwide organization with jurisdiction over all the population of the world.

The woman will then have a terrible lot. The ten kings, symbolized by the ten horns, and the beast will hate her. They will strip her naked, eat her flesh and burn her with fire.

We now learn that it is God, Himself, who brings the ten kings to unity so that they hand their power over to the beast for His prophecy to come to pass.

Chapter 17 ends with the revelation of the identity of the woman – the harlot who sits on many waters: the prostitute is, in fact, ***the great city which reigns over the kings of the earth"***.

As we had guessed, the woman could not be a literal person. We now understand that the word "woman" is used as the personification of a worldwide State – a political, economic and military power. Otherwise, how could her authority extend to the whole world?

The use of the definite article *"the"* to determine the word "city" implies also that the reference is to a specific city – one that stands out among all cities.

And, during the first century when *"Revelation"* was written, if there was a city that had gained more prominence than all the rest, that was Rome. She was, then, at the peak of her fame.

The Roman Empire was extending its tentacles all over Europe and the Middle East. Politically, commercially and militarily, Rome had well and definitely established her supremacy.

In chapter 18, we shall get a much clearer idea of the power designated by the *"woman"* – *"the harlot that sits on many waters"*.

CHAPTER 5

REVELATION 18

_1_ "After these things, I saw another angel coming down out of the sky, having great authority. The earth was illuminated with his glory.

_2_ He cried with a mighty voice, saying, "Fallen, fallen is Babylon the great, and has become a habitation of demons, and a prison of every unclean spirit, and a prison of every unclean and hateful bird!

_3_ For all the nations have drunk of the wine of the wrath of her sexual immorality, the kings of the earth committed sexual immorality with her, and the merchants of the earth grew rich from the abundance of her luxury."

John now sees another angel coming out of the sky. He is an angel having great authority. His is so glorious that his glory illuminates the whole earth.

With a mighty voice, he announces the fall of Babylon the great for it has become a hotbed of every kind of evil and abomination. It has turned into a real habitation for demons and everything that is foul and detestable.

There is a proverb that says: "*What goes up must come down*". We all know also the common phrase: "Rise and Fall".

In the book of the prophet Daniel, we are told that, during the Babylonian captivity, king Nebuchadnezzar – who reigned from 605 BC to 562 BC - had a strange dream.

Upon waking up, however, he had completely forgotten the details of the dream.

Troubled, the king summoned all the kingdom's astrologers and soothsayers. He wanted them to remind him of the details of the dream and interpret its meaning, as well.

Quite naturally, none of them could satisfy the king's requests. If only the king could tell them the dream, they might, perhaps, try to find an explanation to it!

Angered by the astrologers' inability to tell him his dream and explain it to him, the king pronounced a death sentence upon them.

But, fortunately, Daniel – God's prophet – was among the Israelite captives! The Almighty had given him wisdom to interpret dreams for he was a God-fearing and an upright man.

Daniel, therefore, sent word to the king to ask for an opportunity to tell him his dream and explain it. If he succeeded in doing that, he would, thus, save the lives of the soothsayers!

Daniel informed his three companions – Hananiah, Mishael and Azariah – and, together, they sought God's wisdom in prayer. Faithful, the Almighty revealed the secret to His servant Daniel in a vision.

Brought before king, Daniel, in all modesty, did not claim to be personally able to do the king's bidding.

Asked by the king if he could tell him his dream and interpret it,

"*27 Daniel answered before the king, and said, The secret which the king has demanded can neither wise men, enchanters, magicians, nor soothsayers, show to the king;*

28 but there is a God in heaven who reveals secrets, and he has made known to the king Nebuchadnezzar what shall be in the latter days".[60]

Daniel, therefore, told the king that, in his dream, he saw a tall and bizarre statue.

Its head was made of gold, its breast and arms were of silver, its stomach and hips were of

---

[60] Daniel 2: 27-28.

bronze, its legs were of iron and its feet were partly iron and partly clay.

Interpreting the dream, Daniel told the king that the head of pure gold represented himself and his kingdom for, in those days, Babylon was the richest and most powerful kingdom on earth.

The breast and arms of silver represented a lesser kingdom that would arise after Babylon.

Its belly and thighs of brass was a third kingdom that would follow, but that would be less important than the previous one.

Its legs of iron would be yet a lesser power that would next emerge. However, just like iron is hard, this kingdom will crush everything on its path.

Lastly, the feet of iron and clay would be another world power that would come next. But, just like iron and clay are not compatible and do not mix together, so will that last earthly kingdom be fragile. It will end up being divided.

So much for the statue.

But, that was not all! In his dream, the king also saw a little stone: it detached itself from a mountain without the help of any hand and smashed the statue to pieces![61]

Having told the king his dream, Daniel then identified the golden head as Babylon, the greatest power of those day

As for the three other kingdoms that would follow, history has proved that they turned out to be successively Medo-Persia, Greece and Rome.

The last power represented by the feet of iron and clay is deemed by commentators to be a revival of the Roman Empire. The feet may well be revived Rome and the ten toes a coalition of ten European countries. In such a configuration, Rome would, undoubtedly, be the leading figure.

The most intriguing element in Nebuchadnezzar's dream, however, is the

---

[61] Daniel 2: 34.

little stone that detaches itself without any help and smashes the statue to pieces!

That will be the very last Kingdom ever in the whole history of the world. It will be Christ's Eternal Kingdom that will be established on the earth after all other human kingdoms will have been demolished!

If I have referred to the statue in Daniel, it was to show how God has brought low every great human kingdom that has emerged in history.

Most significant of all and most relevant to our present study was the rise and fall of political Babylon. As the saying goes, "The higher the climb, the harder the fall".

But now we are dealing with another Babylon. This one is a religious Babylon – one that is bent upon the destruction of men's souls. One that has spiritually poisoned men's souls with its devil-inspired teachings. One that has engaged into abominable orgies with all the kings of the world. One that has intoxicated them with the wine of its wrath and committed fornication with them.

Of course, this is figurative language. What is implied here is that Babylon is a religious system or organization that has blinded all the people of the world to the truth of God's Word and ensnared them into devil worship.

Babylon is not only a religious organization, but it is also a gigantic commercial network. Indeed, drawn away from the true God, people have enriched themselves thanks to the massive trading going on within the system.

One of the principles God has and that we see throughout the Scriptures is that He never sends punishment or destruction without sending out warning.

Before He sent the Flood, He warned Noah and Noah gave the warning to the people by preaching to them[62].

---

[62] Genesis 6:14. 2 Peter 2:5.

Before He destroyed Sodom, He sent two angels to warn Lot and his household[63].

Before He punished Nineveh, He sent Jonah to preach to them. We remember how Jonah tried to run away from the mission. He got on board a ship bound for Tarsis, instead. But, God brought about circumstances that caused Jonah to be thrown into the sea. The Almighty commanded a large fish to swallow the wayward prophet and throw him up on the shores of Nineveh! Jonah preached to the Ninevites, the people repented and the city was eventually spared.[64]

Likewise, in the New Testament, God sent Jesus to preach the Kingdom of Heaven and redeem mankind by offering Himself as a holy sacrifice.

In turn, Jesus sent out twelve apostles and seventy disciples to spread the Gospel and teach the people how to make peace with

---

[63] Genesis 19: 1-15.
[64] Jonah chapters 1-4.

God through repentance and through Jesus, the Redeemer.

After Jesus's Ascension to Heaven, the Holy Spirit raised other apostles like Paul and Barnabas to take the Gospel to the uttermost parts of the existing world.

Also, before ascending to Heaven, Jesus has given us, His disciples, the Great Commission[65]. In other words, it's our turn now to take up the torch and take the Gospel to the whole world for a witness *"before the end comes"*.

Faithful to His principle and out of mercy, God now gives a final warning to His people:

"4 I heard another voice from heaven, saying, "Come forth, my people, out of her, that you have no participation in her sins, and that you don't receive of her plagues,

5 for her sins have reached to the sky, and God has remembered her iniquities". The command God gives to His people is to leave

---

[65] Matthew 28: 18-20.

Babylon before she is destroyed. The cup of her abominations and adultery overflows and God cannot wait any longer. The Almighty does not want His people to participate in her sins so as not to be struck with the plagues that He will strike her with.

Apart from being adulteress and sinful, Babylon was proud, haughty, self-conceited. She boasted of her wealth and of her luxury.

We remember how pride became the very first sin ever committed in eternity past. Lucifer, the archangel of light whom God created to lead worship in Heaven, one day, grew so proud that he coveted the Almighty's Throne. He wanted to rise above the Almighty. He led a rebellion with a following of one-third of the angelic population, but God cast him and his following out of Heaven and onto the earth.[66]

---

[66] Isaiah 14: 11-17.
Ezekiel 28: 1-8.
Revelation 12: 1-17.

See how Babylon expresses her pride, her self-glorification:

"I sit a queen, and am no widow, and will in no way see mourning" (v 7).

She claims to be sovereign, to be no widow and to never know mourning. She is no widow because she has a legion of lovers – all the kings of the world! She has committed fornication with them all.

Every wrong is a sin. But, if there is one single sin that God hates the most, it's pride – self-glorification! As we have said, that was the very first sin ever committed in Heaven in eternity past. It brought about Lucifer's downfall. Neither will the Almighty suffer pride from anybody else!

The Bible gives us several cases where God broke people's pride and brought them low: the Pharaoh in Exodus, Nebuchadnezzar in Daniel and Herod in Acts[67] – to name but these three.

---

[67] Acts 12: 20-24.

Glory belongs to God only and He won't share it with anybody. Neither will he suffer it from anybody else!

"I am the Lord: that is my name: and my glory will I not give to another, neither my praise to graven images".[68]

Because of her pride and bragging, God is now going to repay Babylon with double of the evil she committed. She will be given the double of the cup of evil wine she gave others to drink.

In one day, she's going to be struck with death, famine, mourning and fire! And those who have committed fornication with her and participated in her lustful and extravagant living will witness, weep and wail over her suffering.

All the kings of the world who fornicated with her will stand afar off and watch the smoke rise as she is consumed by fire.

They will lament over her, saying:

---

[68] Isaiah 42:8, KJV.

"Woe, woe, the great city, Babylon, the strong city! For your judgment has come in one hour" (V.10).

All the merchants who traded with her had enriched themselves. Verses 12-14 list a whole gamut of products and produce that they traded in – haberdashery, precious stones, precious metals, building materials, livestock, grains, fruits, perfumes, sweet smelling plants, military equipment and so on.

In other words, Babylon was so extravagantly rich that she traded in every possible human necessity!

But, among the products she traded in with all the merchants of the world, there are two that really shock us: slaves and, especially, human souls!

It's quite understandable that, standing at a distance, the merchants, who had struck it rich thanks to her, weep, lament and mourn over her destruction, saying:

"16 saying, 'Woe, woe, the great city, she who was dressed in fine linen, purple, and scarlet, and decked with gold and precious stones and pearls!

17 For in an hour such great riches are made desolate".

What follows gives us to understand that Babylon controlled the entire world trade. Indeed, all the ships, sailors, mariners and everybody else engaged in maritime trade keep at a safe distance – for Babylon is burning! – and lament over the loss of their source of revenue. With her, the well of their wealth had run dry!

Still, they stand amazed: *"'What is like the great city?"* they exclaim.

In other words, there never has been a city like her!

Mourning the destruction of Babylon, and in utter desperation, the maritime traders cast dust upon their heads, crying and weeping.

Never would they have thought that such a great and glorious city would be burned down to ashes in just one hour!

Now all Heaven bursts with rejoicing for all the prophets, apostles and other saints who have been persecuted and killed by the dictatorial and God-hating regime of Babylon have been avenged! God has poured out his undiluted wrath upon Babylon!

A mighty angel takes a stone, as big as a millstone, and casts it into the sea to illustrate Babylon's final lot. Just as the stone sinks to the bottom of the sea, so will Babylon be thrown to the greatest depth of the sea, never to be seen again!

Babylon will be dead as dead can be. Not the least music, not the least sound of people working and not the least sound of industry will ever be heard in Babylon or coming from her!

Not the least voice will ever be heard in or coming from Babylon. Nor will the joyous voice of the bride and the bridegroom ever be heard in Babylon. In short, everything that had once made Babylon a great and wealthy city teeming with people, animated with life, bustling with activity and resonating with rejoicing has disappeared for good.

More than death, that is sheer annihilation!

The motives behind such a radical judgment: on one hand, Babylon favoured all the merchants of the world by offering them vast opportunities to enrich themselves even by dealing in slaves and in human souls while, on the other hand, she persecuted, killed and martyred God's holy servants and saints.

Thus, Babylon is no exception to the law of sowing and harvesting. She sowed suffering, blood, death, immorality, she now harvests complete annihilation. She gave to the world the cup of abominations and of the wine of her sexual immorality[69] to drink; now she's given the cup of God's wrath in return.

---

[69] Revelation 17: 4.

CHAPTER 6

REVELATION 19

1 After these things I heard something like a loud voice of a great multitude in heaven, saying, "Hallelujah! Salvation, glory, and power belong to our God:

2 for true and righteous are his judgments. For he has judged the great prostitute, her who corrupted the earth with her sexual immorality, and he has avenged the blood of his servants at her hand."

3 A second time they said, "Hallelujah! Her smoke goes up forever and ever."

Now that Babylon the Great has fallen, there is great rejoicing in Heaven.

John hears a great multitude – surely of angels and other heavenly beings – declaring, with a loud voice, that salvation, power and glory belong to God, and offering praise to Him. They confirm that His judgments are just, right and well deserved for, in all fair justice, He has judged Babylon, the great harlot, who persecuted and shed the blood of His saints. Also, she had corrupted the whole earth – which is God's creation - with her immorality.

The Bible says: *"Don't be deceived. God is not mocked, for whatever a man sows, that will he also reap."*[70]

In parading her pride and her luxury so haughtily, in shamelessly committing such glaring immorality with all the kings of the earth, in corrupting the whole world, and in shedding the blood of God's saints, she had provoked God's anger and incurred His just judgment.

---

[70] Galatians 6:7.

"For we know him who said, "Vengeance belongs to me," says the Lord."[71]

And the heavenly creatures rejoice and give glory to God for the smoke of burning Babylon that rises forever and ever.

In *"Revelation"* chapters 4 and 5, we saw that, around God's Throne in Heaven, there were twenty-four elders and four living creatures.[72] Their ministry is to worship the Almighty and give glory to Him whenever something dramatic or glorious happens in Heaven.

Accordingly, to celebrate God's victory over Babylon the Great, the twenty-four Elders and the four living creatures bow down and worship the Almighty.

Following that, the apostle John hears a loud voice calling for everybody else who serves God to raise their voices and glorify Him.

Thereupon, a very loud voice – like many waters and many thunders – is heard,

---

[71] Hebrews 13:10.
[72] Revelation Revisited, Volume 1.

magnifying God and proclaiming His reign. It must be the myriads and myriads of angels – like a heavenly choir – giving glory to God, all in one accord. They invite everybody to be glad and rejoice for the Wedding Supper of the Lamb has come and His Bride is ready.

The scope of this volume ends here. Its aims were to examine the judgments of the seven bowls of God's wrath and to try to understand the mystery of Babylon the Great.

We shall, therefore, look deeper into the subject of the Wedding Supper of the Lamb in the next volume.

However, this volume would be incomplete without a reflection on the subject of Babylon the Great.

That is what we shall do now before closing.

CHAPTER 7

WHO OR WHAT IS BABYLON THE GREAT?

"8 Therefore he says, "When he [Jesus] ascended on high, he led captivity captive, and gave gifts to men."

11 He gave some to be apostles; and some, prophets; and some, evangelists; and some, shepherds and teachers;

12 for the perfecting of the saints, to the work of serving, to the building up of the body of Christ;

13 until we all attain to the unity of the faith, and of the knowledge of the Son of God, to a full grown man, to the measure of the stature of the fullness of Christ;

<u>14</u> that we may no longer be children, tossed back and forth and carried about with every wind of doctrine, by the trickery of men, in craftiness, after the wiles of error"[73]

"*<u>16</u> Every writing inspired by God is profitable for teaching, for reproof, for correction, and for instruction which is in righteousness,*

<u>17</u> that the man of God may be complete, thoroughly equipped for every good work"[74].

The reason for my placing those two Scriptures at the head of this chapter is to establish the Biblical foundation on which I base myself to preach and teach God's Word.

The above clearly says that it is the Risen Christ who has given certain specific ministries to the Church. These four or five

---

[73] Ephesians 4: 8-14.
[74] 2 Timothy 3: 16-17.

ministry gifts are apostles, prophets, evangelists, pastors and teachers.

Why four or five? Well, some believe that pastors and teachers are one and the same ministry. In a sense it's true because pastors are supposed to be teachers of the Word, as well, because they are called upon to feed the flock[75].

But I doubt if all teachers can be pastors. I, for one, am a teacher. I have many a time been offered a church to pastor, but I have always declined. I do not have the managerial competence to take charge of a church nor to administer pastoral care on a continual basis.

Moreover, the ministry of a teacher must be an itinerant one. He may often be invited by other churches to teach sound doctrine.

My personal interpretation goes in favour of five ministry gifts for the reasons I have just mentioned.

---

[75] John 21: 15-17.
1 Peter 5: 1-4.

The above Scriptures also tell us the purpose behind these ministries. They have been given to certain specific people to edify the believers – that is, to bring them up and help them grow spiritually so that they do not remain children and fall prey to all kinds of false doctrines. The ministries are also meant to prepare believers, who have grown in the Word, to start serving the LORD, as well. Finally, the ministries have to bring unity within the body of believers.

The Scriptures taken from 2 Timothy 3:16 also go in the same direction. They confirm and support the Scriptures taken from Ephesians.

The reason why I have elaborated to some length on these Scriptures is to protect my rearguard. I want to make it clear that I do not mean to be offensive in what I am going to say in this chapter. My calling is to preach and teach the Word of God.

The central theme of the New Testament – of the whole Bible, in fact – is John 3:16:

"For God so loved the world that He gave His only begotten Son so that whoever believes in Him shall not perish, but have eternal life".

Indeed, God loves everybody. He loves all peoples and all people. He has proved it by offering His only Son, Jesus, as a living sacrifice for the redemption of our souls.

Catholics are no exception: God loves them, as well.

I, myself, was born in a Roman Catholic family. Most of my relatives are still Catholic. I daily pray for them to come to the Lord, and testify to them whenever the opportunity occurs.

I have also many friends and acquaintances in the Catholic Church. I love them all and would rejoice to see them confessing Jesus Christ as their personal Saviour and Lord.

Allow me, please, to offer a short prayer for all Catholics before I continue.

"Heavenly Father, I know you love every single person on earth. We are all your creation. You love the Catholics, too, just as you love everybody else. You have given your Son Jesus to die for them and for us alike. Help them Father, to read this chapter with an open mind. May your Holy Spirit open their intelligence and give them wisdom so that they will know the truth that sets them free[76] and let them know that your Son Jesus is the way, the truth and the life;[77] and that no-one comes to you, except through Him. In Jesus's Name I pray. Thank you, Father. Amen."

Who or what is Babylon the Great? What is the mystery behind that enigmatic figure?

These questions and other similar ones have often been asked by various Bible

---

[76] John 8: 32.
[77] John 14:6.

commentators. But there is no consensus concerning the answer – at least as far as certain details are concerned.

But, let's not forget that the Biblical book that speaks about Babylon the Great is called "*Revelation*" and that a revelation is an unveiling.

"*1 This is the Revelation of Jesus Christ, which God gave him to show to his servants the things which must happen soon, which he sent and made known by his angel to his servant, John.*"[78]

Those are the opening words of the Book of Revelation.

The Risen Lord Jesus did not appear to the apostle John on the Isle of Patmos to tell him to obscure and occult everything: instead, He wanted John to write in order to "*show*" and to "*make known*"!

It is, therefore, clear that "*Revelation*" reveals – unveils, uncovers, demystifies.

____

[78] Revelation 1:1.

This does not mean that we may know each and every detail regarding Babylon the Great. We must understand that much of "*Revelation*" is figurative language. Also, it contains certain images and symbols of *that* time and of *that* region which may not be intelligible to us, modern men and women of the twenty-first century.

Nevertheless, we cannot deny that "*Revelation*" reveals much that, with the help of history, we can reasonably understand.

Let's see how much of Babylon the Great we can understand – without, however, being dogmatic about it.

To begin with, it is generally accepted that "*Revelation*" was written in 95-96 CE. During the first century, the political power that was reigning over the world was the Roman Empire. Rome was, indeed, the capital of the world of that time.

Under the Roman Emperors, Christians were ruthlessly persecuted. They were arrested, imprisoned, tortured, killed, fed to lions, crucified, hanged head down and burnt alive. The Roman Emperors so hated the Christians that they devised the cruelest ways to kill them by inflicting to them the most excruciating suffering ….

The only "crimes" of the Christians were that they refused to renounce their faith and practise Caesar worship. Indeed, Emperors considered themselves to be gods and commanded worship of them.

It is well known that Nero, in his folly, set fire to Rome and blamed it on the Christians. That event took place in 64 AD and is known as the Great Fire of Rome.[79]

Babylon is identified as a woman sitting on seven mountains (17.9). Somehow, Rome

---

[79] Wikipedia: Persecution of Christians in the Roman Empire. Accessed 9 February 2024.

Britannica, The Editors of Encyclopaedia. "Nero". Encyclopedia Britannica, 11 Dec. 2023, https://www.britannica.com/biography/Nero-Roman-emperor. Accessed 9 February 2024.

Wikipedia: Great Fire of Rome. Accessed 09/02/2024.

happens to be the only city situated on seven hills: Aventine, Caelian, Capitoline, Esquiline, Palatine, Quirinal and Viminal.[80]

It is also said that the woman sits over many waters (17:1). The Scriptures define the "many waters" a peoples, multitudes, nations and languages (17:15).

Which political power was reigning over the world of that time? Which political power had peoples, races and nations under its jurisdiction? Of course, it was, without contest, the Roman Empire.

The woman is referred to as a prostitute[81]. Many cities were called "prostitutes" in the Old Testament: Nineveh[82], Tyre,[83] and, even, Jerusalem.[84]

---

[80] Britannica, The Editors of Encyclopaedia. "Seven Hills of Rome". Encyclopedia Britannica, 13 Jun. 2023, https://www.britannica.com/place/Seven-Hills-of-Rome. Accessed 9 February 2024.
[81] Revelation 17: 1; 17: 16.
[82] Nahum 3:4.
[83] Isaiah 23: 17.
[84] Isaiah 1: 21.

The main reason God calls a city a prostitute is that that city turns away from Him and worships idols and pagan gods. This is spiritual prostitution.

Why, then, should Babylon the Great be called a prostitute?

It is clear from chapters 17 and 18 that the modern Babylon is a religious organization, as well. She has given to all nations the wine of the wrath of her immorality to drink (18:3). In other words, religious Babylon – much more than the Jezebel in Thyatira[85] – has introduced and taught many false doctrines to her followers. She has intoxicated them spiritually.

The woman wears a scarf with the following words in block letters;

""MYSTERY, BABYLON THE GREAT, THE MOTHER OF THE PROSTITUTES AND OF THE ABOMINATIONS OF THE EARTH" (17:5).

---

[85] Revelation 2: 20-23.

In ancient Rome, prostitutes sometimes wore a headband with their name on it so as to advertise their profession.

The woman is said to be dressed in purple and scarlet (17:3). In the ancient world, purple was worn by Roman magistrates, by the rulers of the Byzantine Empire and by the Roman Emperors. it's a colour associated with royalty.

In Luke 16, Jesus speaks of a rich man dressed in purple in fine linen.[86]

The Book of Acts also mentions a woman called Lydia who was a seller of purple. Her heart was touched by the preaching of God's word and she became a believer.[87]

With time, purple has become the characteristic of Roman Catholic Bishops. At any great Roman Catholic ceremony, purple is the dominant colour.

The proverb says: *"All roads lead to Rome"*.

---

[86] Luke 16: 19-31.
[87] Acts 16:14.

As we see in examining Babylon the Great, all evidence leads … to Rome!

We have seen that Babylon is not only a mighty political and commercial power, but it is also a religious organization.

The political characteristic of Babylon the Great will, undoubtedly, be a revival of the Roman Empire. Remember the beast whose fatal wound was healed[88].

The revived Roman Empire will, perhaps, be at the head of a coalition of ten countries symbolized by the ten toes of the statue in Daniel. That coalition may have been typified by the leg of iron and feet of clay of the statue.

But what about the religious aspect of Babylon? What major religion appears to be the likeliest prospect to be the religious "wing" of Babylon?

Well, the one religion that is based in Rome is the Catholic Church. Its headquarters are

---

[88] Revelation 13:3.

in the City of Vatican in Rome. The Vatican is, itself, a State within the State of Italy. It is the smallest State in the world – but how powerful and how rich!

During the days of the Roman Empire, Christians were martyred by most Emperors, such as Claudius, Nero, Domitian, Trajan and others.

Throughout history, the Catholic Church has persecuted and killed thousands of Christians.

During the sixteenth century, the Papacy was teaching salvation by works. Pope Leo X was sending agents all over Germany and in Europe to sell Indulgences – that is, an absolution of sins. Prospective buyers could either have their sins forgiven and go to Heaven after death, or have their "sentence" reduced so they could spend less time in Purgatory and go to Heaven sooner.

Purgatory, by the way, is an unbiblical, unscriptural teaching. Nowhere is the word mentioned in the Bible nor the concept thereof.

When Johann Tetzel, the Pope's agent, came to Wittenberg to sell Indulgences, that enraged Martin Luther, a monk. Luther, who was studying Theology at Doctorate level, recognized that monumental error for the Bible teaches that salvation is by Grace alone and not by works. One cannot obtain one's justification by works or personal merit.[89]

Consequently, Luther wrote down Ninety-Five Theses and, on 31 October 1517, he nailed them on the door of the castle church in Wittenberg.

That brought about his excommunication from the Catholic Church and the birth of Protestantism. That event marked the breaking away from Rome and has been called the Great Reformation.

---

[89] Ephesians 2: 5.
Galatians 4: 7.

Thanks to the invention of the printing press by Gutenberg[90], the wind of protest spread all over Europe through John Calvin in France, Zwingli in Switzerland, John Knox in Scotland, John and Charles Wesley in England.

Following that great breaking away from Rome, generalized persecution began.

One date, however, has remained a real landmark in the history of Protestants' persecution by Catholics: the night of August 24-25, 1572!

On that night – St. Bartholomew's night - the church bells rang to signal the beginning of the massacre of Huguenots – French Protestants. The plot was fomented by Queen Catherine de' Medici and executed by French nobles.

The Huguenots' houses and businesses were destroyed and pillaged. People were

---

[90] Lehmann-Haupt, Hellmut E.. "Johannes Gutenberg". Encyclopedia Britannica, 31 Jan. 2024, https://www.britannica.com/biography/ Johannes-Gutenberg. Accessed 9 February 2024.

ruthlessly slaughtered and their bodies thrown into the Seine. Rivers of blood flowed in the streets of Paris.

According to an estimate by a Catholic apologist, 2,000 people were killed. But that figure is heavily biased. On the other hand, a witness of the event – the Huguenot Maximilien de Béthune, duc de Sully, places the figure at 70,000. Even if we argue that his estimate is also biased, his figure must better reflect the reality for he was a contemporary and, himself, "barely escaped death".

According to modern estimates, about 3,000 were slaughtered in Paris only.[91]

That God-fearing Christians have been persecuted and savagely put to death since the times of the Roman Empire throughout

---

[91] Britannica, The Editors of Encyclopaedia. "Massacre of St. Bartholomew's Day". Encyclopedia Britannica, 18 Jan. 2024, https://www.britannica.com/event/Massacre-of-Saint-Bartholomews-Day. Accessed 9 February 2024.

the centuries is a fact that can be easily verified.

That is what Revelation 17 and 18 refer to when they say:

"*6 I saw the woman drunken with the blood of the saints, and with the blood of the martyrs of Jesus*" [17:6].

"*24 In her was found the blood of prophets and of saints, and of all who have been slain on the earth.*" [18:24].

But what about the immorality, the prostitution, the harlotry that the woman has committed with the kings of the world and with which she has intoxicated the nations of the world?

Which religion has corrupted God's Word the most? While the Bible teaches very clearly that justification is by faith and grace alone, which religion has placed its teachings at par with God's Word? Which religion has replaced God's Commandments by traditions? Which religion has introduced a number of false doctrines – such as

Mariolatry, prayers to dead "saints", the Purgatory, the Rosary, the Sign of the Cross, Ash Wednesday and so on?

The list is, indeed, very long. None of the above doctrines is found in the Holy Scriptures. Yet, they are taught and practised in Roman Catholicism.

"7 But in vain do they worship me, Teaching as doctrines the commandments of men.'

8 "For you set aside the commandment of God, and hold tightly to the tradition of men -- the washing of pitchers and cups, and you do many other such things."

9 He said to them, "Full well do you reject the commandment of God, that you may keep your tradition.[92]

Since some time now, world leaders have been talking about the establishment of a New World Order. Their aim is to place the

---

[92] Mark 7: 7-9.

whole world under one government with a leader lording it over the whole world.

Would you be surprised if I told you that the word *"catholic"* means *"universal"*?

It means also *"broad in sympathies, tastes, or interests"* [93]

"Oecumenism" - also spelt Ecumenism[94] - is a term used to refer to the coming together of all "Christian" churches for greater support and unity among them. That movement stated in 1937 and led to the establishment of the World Council of Churches.[95]

However, we now see a broadening of this group so that we see "Christians" joining together with Hindus, Muslims and

---

[93] Catholic: COMPREHENSIVE, UNIVERSAL *especially*: broad in sympathies, tastes, or interests a *catholic* taste in music (Merriam-Webster).

[94] CAMBRIDGE DICTIONARY: Ecumenical: A:encouraging the different Christian Churches to unite:

[95] Wikipedia: Ecumenism. Accessed 9 February 2024.

Buddhists, claiming that "all religions lead to God".

Most of these religions reject the deity of Christ while Jesus, Himself, says:

"I am the way, the truth and the life. No-one comes to the Father, but by me" [96]

That attempt at bringing unity among all world religions explains why *"ecumenism"* means *"broad in sympathies, tastes, or interests"*. It's a movement that tends to blend all religions in one.

If we refer to the statue in Daniel 2, we shall remember that, after Babylon, Medo-Persia, Greece and Rome, there appeared another kingdom represented by the iron leg and feet of clay.

Most probably, that kingdom will be a revival of the Roman Empire typified by the beast whose *"fatal wound was healed"*[97]. As

---

[96] John 14: 6.
[97] Revelation 13: 3.

for the ten toes, of clay, that may well be a coalition of European countries.

Just as the ten kings gave their power to the Beast, so will the ten countries surrender their power to the Beast [17:12-13].

As for the Beast, if he is to rule over the whole world, he will have to be a charismatic personage – one who will be a political as well as a religious leader.

As *"Revelation"* says: *"Here is the mind that has wisdom"* [17:9].

With reference to the statue in Daniel 2, remember that John saw a small stone that detached itself from a mountain without the help of any hand and smashed the statue to pieces.

 Let's see what this means.

Eventually, this mega coalition, led by the Beast, will wage war with Jesus and His faithful ones. But Jesus will defeat them for He is Lord of lords and King of kings [17:14].

That small stone represents Jesus who will defeat the Beast and his army and, eventually, establish His Eternal Kingdom.

Thus, after all human kingdoms – no matter how great and how powerful - will have failed, Jesus will establish his Eternal Kingdom on Earth and reign with His Saints.

What a metamorphosis that will be! After all the hatred, the violence, the fighting, the bloodshed and the immorality that have plagued the world, Christ will establish His Eternal Reign of peace, justice, love and perfect harmony!

But, before that happens, there are a few events that must first take place.

Those will constitute the subject of our next volume.

ABOUT THE AUTHOR

Jean Norbert Augustin was born in 1948 in a Roman Catholic family.

He went to Curepipe Boys' Government School for his primary education.

Then he had his secondary education at Mauritius College and Union College.

After that, he studied for a General Certificate of Education with Cambridge University (England).

In 1966, while he was still a student at Union College, his Manager offered to employ him as a teacher as soon as he would receive his exam results. Accordingly, the following year, he joined the Union College teaching staff as French language and literature teacher.

While he was already in his teaching post, he studied part-time for a Teaching Certificate with the Mauritius Institute of Education.

Eventually, he obtained his Teacher's Certificate with Merit.

In 1971, Union College was taken over by Presidency College. The author, however, stayed on the staff until his retirement in 2008.

Thereafter, he was offered a teaching job at Mauricia Institute – a private fee-paying college belonging to a close friend.

Altogether, he spent 52 years, teaching French and, occasionally, English.

In 1982, he was born again in the Assemblies of God.

In 1983, he was called to the ministry and, to this day, he has been serving the Body of Christ in the capacity of an Evangelist-Teacher.

Married, he has two adult children and four grandsons.

He holds a Diploma in Principles of Modern Management, a Christian Broadcaster's Certificate – Grade A, a Lyricist Certificate

(USA), a Doctorate in Divinity and a Doctorate in Missionary Ministries.

He has published the following books:

Bought and Bonded by Blood

The Day Justice Was Judged

From Teacher to Preacher (Autobiography)

Voices from the Cloud (Poetry)

In Quest of Truth (Memoir)

Fatal Success (Novella)

Revelation Revisited – Volumes 1- 4

Long Live Love (Novel).